Always on Fire

Milton J Bates

Always on Fire

Milton J. Bates

Five Oaks Press
FIVE-OAKS-PRESS.COM

Copyright ©2016 Milton J. Bates
All rights reserved. First print edition

Five Oaks Press
Newburgh, NY 12550
five-oaks-press.com
editor@five-oaks-press.com

ISBN: 978-1-944355-12-8

Cover Art: Milton J. Bates

Printed in the United States of America

Acknowledgments

This collection includes a poem that first appeared in the anthology *Encore: Prize Poems 2015*. Others appeared in the following magazines: *Dunes Review*, *Fire Tetrahedron*, *Great Lakes Review*, *Midwestern Gothic*, *Peninsula Poets*, *The Southern Review*, and *Stirring*.

Contents

Supposing the House Is on Fire	5
The Darkroom	6
Bereft	7
Waking to Cranes	8
Listening to September	9
Road Kill Retro-Loop	10
Lost and Found	11
Lake Superior Levitations: Winter	12
Breakfast at the Huron Mountain Bakery	14
Transmigration	16
Sublimation	17
Superior Ice-Out	18
Skeleton Found in Ore Dock 6	19
Totaled	21
Animal Faith	22
Windbound with Dostoevsky	23
A Twilight Moonrise	24
Forty-Six Degrees North	25

Supposing the House Is on Fire

It's a game we play. *Suppose the house is
on fire*, we say. *What would you try to save?*
Our children aren't for saving anymore.
They've grown up and moved to houses of their own.
No pets either, to complicate the choice.

You open with the jeans you'd grab because
you've never had a pair that fit so well.
I counter with my lucky fishing rod.
We're just warming up, passing the time
until one of us plays the winning card,
the same one every game. We'd rescue our
photos first, low-crawling through smoky rooms,
dodging the falling embers and sparking wires
because we can't bear to lose the story
pictures tell, the proof we've walked this earth.

We tried a retrospective once, gorging
nightly on prints and slides, devouring
digital images. We remarked how young
we looked, how peculiar our clothes,
how we really must return to destination
x or y. The surfeit left us still unsatisfied.

What's missing from the record? we asked
ourselves, and had to answer, *almost everything*.
It's a game we play, the picture-taking too.
Who'd ever guess that we sipped coffee
as the sun came up, spent most days working,
touched each other in the dark? Pictures
don't lie. But they keep secrets, including
this one: the house is always on fire.

The Darkroom

When he needed to see things clearly,
he retreated to a walled-off corner
of the basement, switched on a red light,

and poured potions from brown bottles into trays.
Then he fed a filmstrip into the enlarger
and twisted the lens until his world snapped

into focus. It wasn't as he remembered
it, not yet, but the photo paper's
silver salts would make it right again,

turn black to white and white to black. He threw
an image onto the light-shy surface,
counted down, and eased it into a tray.

A picture bloomed in the seiche-like sloshing
of developer. He bathed it in fresh water,
locked it in with fixer, and rinsed it off.

Under white light the likeness seemed true
enough, but not as true as one he'd glimpsed
before the grays turned black. He'd heard

of images like that, shimmering above
the polar ice or desert sand. Shapes that weren't
quite there. Things seen once, seen truly,

never seen again. He hung the print
to dry and climbed the stairs to daylight,
climbed slowly toward that other darkness.

Bereft, He Chooses a Grave Marker

Stone
would not do, granite or marble polished
to give back a face he knew too well,
etched with grief. Fine-grained as glass
or steel, impervious, it would tell
his fingertips too much, too soon,
about the permanence of loss.

Wood
it would have to be, red oak from a tree
like those that framed her garden. It would
weather like their marriage. It would need
attention. He'd massage it weekly
with fragrant oil, feeling in its grain
the familiar texture of her skin.

Earth
would claim him too, so he'd have another
ready for himself. With no one
to anoint them the slabs would check
and warp, turn gray and crumble
into dust. This he could foresee.
This was how it had to be.

Waking to Cranes

He couldn't tell at first what woke him.
Then he heard it again, the unearthly,
rattling trumpet call of sandhill cranes.
He could almost see them through the roof,
their great wings working, their long legs trailing
as they made their way by moonlight to the Gulf.

He was canoeing a river with his wife
when he'd seen them for the first time, a red-capped
pair guarding a nest among the cattails.
They're older than we are, he'd whispered,
by millions of years. Their age had mattered less
to her. *They mate for life,* she'd whispered back.

For life, he thought, smoothing the sheet beside him.
When the sun came up he'd walk as usual
through an unmowed meadow to the cemetery.
The daisies and black-eyed susans would be
shriveled up by now, not worth the picking.
But he might still find a patch of bee-balm,
shaking its crimson pompoms in the dry grass.

Listening to September

Our noisy summer guests have slipped away
without so much as a goodbye,
leaving local residents to wonder
whether the place is really theirs again.
A chickadee tries out a riff we haven't heard
since spring, then stops to listen. What it hears,
we hear too: a peeper's high-pitched note,
sounding at intervals day and night.
In May that soloist was one of many
in a grand chorale. A gray tree frog chimes in
now and then, squeezing from the bagpipe
at its throat a deeper, reedy trill. Are these
the die-hards, not quite ready to call it
a season? Or youngsters trying out
for parts in next summer's ensemble?
Soon the frost will slow their pulses too,
and mute their music. They'll burrow
under leaves and listen like the rest of us
for the chickadee's breezy wakeup call.

Road Kill Retro-Loop

Except for a seething rice of maggots,
the twisted rag of fur and flesh
lies still beside the highway, *nature morte*.

Then the implausible happens:
ravens land and drop the eyes back in,
lustrous black and fat as plums.

The coat zips up and swells with meat.
Enamel brightens on the teeth.
The hooves glisten with wet lacquer.

A bloody ten-yard smear connects
the carcass to a car speeding in reverse,
its headlights diminishing to pinpricks.

The creature takes the impact in mid-stride.
Then with hind legs levering backwards
it retreats tail-first into the woods.

There it pauses, looking past the highway
toward a moonlit trail leading to a cornfield.
The plum-eyed doe can see exactly

where it has to go. It levers forward
on its haunches, steps onto the pavement,
and takes the impact in mid-stride.

Lost and Found

Shorts, T-shirt, sneakers, shower stuff:
all there in my gym bag, but not
the combination lock. I've left it
on a locker door before, so I know
where to go. The woman behind
the counter pulls out a cardboard box
full mostly of Master Locks.
Their numbered, nearly identical
faces look up at me like orphan
children hoping for adoption.
Lost and Found, I say, pointing to
hand-printed letters on the box.
Which ones are found? She gives me
that look reserved for smart alecks,
but she's glad to have a job at the Y,
so she answers, *only one—the one
you're able to open.* I rattle through
the locks, trying those that look beat-up
enough to be mine. Spin the dial to 5,
turn counterclockwise past the 5 to 12,
then clockwise to 46. At last one clicks
at 46. Out slides the shackle, easy
as the well-oiled bolt on my .22.
I smile at the woman, and she
smiles back, her theory confirmed:
lost things can't find themselves. They need
a finder's familiar touch to open,
to be again what they were meant to be.

Lake Superior Levitations: Winter

i. Moonrise

Someone lights a lamp
in an igloo where
polar ice and sky
converge. The dome is
veined with gray and blue.

Through night's dark tunnel
the Trans-Siberian
Express approaches.
Its single Cyclops
eye reddens the rails.

A silver coin hangs
in space, suspended.
Heads or tails? There'll be
no winners tonight,
no losers either.

ii. Sunrise

A barn is burning
on the horizon.
Its flames extinguish
stars and warm the ice
from blue to salmon.

A mob ran riot
through the streets, smashing
windows. Shards lie strewn
about, reflecting
or transmitting light.

Shadows and rabbits
retreat to snow caves.
Smudging the whiteness,
a lone coyote
makes it whiter still.

Breakfast at the Huron Mountain Bakery

They face each other across the table
like opposing linemen, their heads
tucked into hunched shoulders,
their fists gripping coffee mugs.

It's always the same table,
a booth that commands a view
of parked cars. The patient grills
stand in formation, looking back.

At the front counter we share
a smile of recognition as we pay
for our coffee, redeye as usual,
and the usual toasted bagels.

Some things never change:
the coffee, the bagels,
the soft-eyed woman who
fetches them before we can order.

Also, of course, the Loud Guy
and his friend. *So whaddya think
of the new millage? Where will
it end?* Too loud, much too loud.

The room holds its breath
as though the answer matters.
The friend's mouth moves
inaudibly. What does he think?

Where will it end?
His half-hearing partner

nods, reading answers in
the pantomime of lip and brow.

Beyond the ranked grills,
well beyond, rises the knob
for which this place was named.
Forged in fire and ice,

it's been quiet a long time.
The Loud Guy, too, will be
quiet for a long time.
Some things do change.

This morning, though,
he's still in full voice.
Sliding into our booth, the usual,
we silently cheer him on.

Transmigration

To the jay it must have seemed as though
a thunderbolt had struck it from its perch.
It lay in the snow beneath the feeder, stunned,

after the other birds dispersed. So many eyes,
yet none had seen the dark comet coming
through the balsams. The chosen one resisted

briefly as the sharp-shin's talons probed its breast
and throat. Then it relaxed, its black eyes
focused on the distance like a martyr

or jihadist contemplating paradise.
It hardly felt the beak that rummaged
through its down and ripped its belly open.

Shifting its grip, the hawk hauled out
the smoking viscera, tugging as a robin
tugs at earthworms. It dipped repeatedly

for meat, for heat, for fluid in a frozen world.
Bit by bit one life became another.
What lifted off and flew away was neither

hawk nor jay but both, a mythic bird.
A plaque of feathers marks the place of rapture,
sky-blue with dabs of black and white.

Sublimation

> *We travel the Milky Way together,*
> *trees and men.*
> —John Muir

The orange, air-starved flame inside
my woodstove paints the window black.
When the stove gets hot enough to sear
the contour lines from fingertips,

that soot will turn to spirit, ghost
of red oak, and fly up the chimney.
Two years split and stacked, the wood's
well seasoned, full of all it drank

from soil and air: carbon from
a bygone season's leaves and acorns,
carbon from the power plant upwind,
where black rocks burn to light my house.

The glass begins to clear. I picture
the big white pine that looms above
my chimney, leaning in as though
to warm its boughs, inhaling CO_2.

That pine has saved up several tons
of carbon. I'm good for thirty pounds
in flesh and bone. It's ours to keep, man
and tree, till fire turns us both to ghosts.

Superior Ice-Out

Living by the lake, we don't trust returning
birds to tell us winter's over. We watch
the ice and listen. For weeks we've heard
it whoop and detonate offshore, seen
the plates it's piled into windrows. More
docile now, it fractures quietly along
its fault lines. Water shows like ink between
snow-dusted geometric panels—squares,
rectangles, diamonds, trapezoids.
Then a wind disturbs the slabs, smudging
the neatly ruled lines. We look away,
distracted for a moment by less
momentous goings-on, then look back
to find the landscape rearranged. The sheets
are gone, replaced by what? Dragon scales?
Acres of honeycomb? Salt craters from
a dried-up sea? Freighter pilots call it
pancake ice, making of our flesh-numbing lake
a flesh-searing griddle. The cakes crunch
and jostle, fizz and tinkle, their edges
growing rounder as they socialize.

That's our cue to creep from winter houses,
to blink in the mid-March sun like hostages
released. We walk our dogs and check our
mailboxes, bumping into neighbors
who look familiar, remembered from
another time and place. Our voices sound
unnatural when we stop to talk, a bit
too loud, as though we're trying to be heard
above the slosh and sizzle of the ice.

Skeleton Found in Ore Dock 6

i. October 19, 1988

Halfway down chute 18 it hangs
like a cocoon waiting for spring
to trigger the transformation
plotted in the larval DNA.

But this is fall, and the raveled
chrysalis of parka, jeans,
and tennis shoes, derelict as
the dock itself, holds only bones.

Two summers have cooked the juices
off. Two winters have freeze-dried
the skin and meat. Empty sockets
stare unbelieving upward

at the catwalk that gave his feet
the slip. Today two boys intrepid
as he was but more sure-footed
will find a missing person

before he's even missed. He'll be
a one-week wonder in the news,
delivered nameless and stillborn
from Number 6's rusty loins.

ii. April 1986

When he stepped from the hotel porch
onto Spring Street, he left it all
behind: the months in foster care,
the miles of pointless wandering

between Mount Clemens and Marquette.
Left or right? The rising sun drew
him toward the lake, for it was spring
despite the soiled rags of snow.

He could feel the randy buzz
of new beginning in his bones.
Today he'd slough Tim Allain off,
lose that loser's wasted years, all

seventeen. Ahead, colossal
legs and hips rose from the water,
inviting him to mount and enter,
daring him to be reborn.

Totaled

Stepping from the car unscathed, I looked first
at where the road dropped off to blasted rock,
then back at the cedar posts strung like fish
on steel cable. How many had my Subaru
uprooted? The tow truck driver counted
seventeen, said it was a local record.

My Subie joined the wrecks at his garage,
another crumpled ball around the basket.
When I came inside to call insurance,
he handed me his card. Above his name
and number was an upbeat motto:
We meet the nicest folks by accident.

Waiting for my agent to pick up, I thought
of those I'd met—the woman who stopped
to see if I was hurt, the cop she called for help,
the tow truck driver. Nice folks, every one,
but the nicest were those I'll never meet,
the crew that rigged a safety net between
that highway and whatever lies beyond.

Animal Faith

If God is a merganser—and who's to say
He isn't?—our nesting pair may get a break
this year. Last spring they discovered
the big birch a storm decapitated long ago,
leaving the white column of its trunk to weather
like the last pillar of a Roman temple.

Rain and snow, freeze and thaw, mold and rot
scooped out a nest-sized hollow at the top.
The birds trimmed it out with feathers,
laid a clutch of eggs, and settled in to wait.

Their holidays were few and much the same,
a giddy glide from nest to lake, landing
with the kind of splash you have to pay for
at a water park. The trick was how to come
and go without disclosing an address.
Nature loves guile as much as patience.

They seemed to have the knack. An eagle
hunted daily from a dead snag at their doorstep,
unsuspecting. Then one day the snag was full
of crows, converging like gangsters on a bank.
That's how we knew the eggs had hatched,
that crows are smarter than eagles and mergansers.

Will the mob show up again this year,
shrugging their thuggish shoulders on the snag?
Our ducks take turns on the water slide.
They skim the lake for minnows and insects.
They are devious and patient, confiding
in a providence we find inscrutable.
We trust in our God too, our money says so,
but we have our reservations. Come hatching
time, we'll see which species got it right.

Windbound with Dostoevsky

June 2012

When Duluth flooded and zoo animals
drowned, the polar bear escaped. Before it
fell to a drug-tipped dart, it gave city folk
the frisson of a wilder place. The storm,
undarted, lumbered north and east across
the big lake, where it caught up with us.

We beached our kayaks and pitched our tent,
then rolled into fetal balls and played dead.
All night the thunder growled and lightning
clawed the sky. The worst of it was gone
by morning, hunting other prey. We woke
to the soft chatter of rain on nylon.

What better time for Dostoevsky?
All day his story of Muishkin, the gentle
prince misnamed The Idiot, unfolded
in our tent. When the rain stopped I took it
with me to the shore. Did stone and water
care that Nastasia lay dead in the ruins
of her wedding dress? That Rogojin
would do hard labor for her murder?
That the prince was once again an infant?

Superior still churned when I closed the book,
as though trying to scrub the human pain
from granite walls. Would they be clean by morning?
If so, the lake might have us back. We'd rise
refreshed, illiterate as serfs, and paddle on.

A Twilight Moonrise

In memory of John Dapra

The chairs are still there, John, but the magic
is gone. Gliding past them in my kayak,
I recall how you performed, one summer

evening, a moonrise over Lake Superior.
Through ferns and bunchberries you led the way
to a sandstone mezzanine already set

with wine and cheese. We waited—Puck and I,
you and Karen—for the theatre lights to dim.
You checked your watch once, twice, and then, maestro,

it seemed as though the spectral disk emerged
on the downbeat of your baton. *Voilà
la lune!* You acknowledged our applause as

your star attraction lifted red and ripe
above the horizon. That was ten years
ago. You'd think that someone who controls

the moon could handle anything, could even
dodge the pitch that got Lou Gehrig. Today
the chairs are yours no longer, nor the house.

The magic too is gone, except on summer
evenings when that other wizard rises from
the lake and conjures up your memory.

Forty-Six Degrees North

> *There is nothing to do, nowhere to get.*
> *We need only "stand still in the light."*
> —Theodore Roszak

On those autumn days
when there is nothing to do
after the firewood is stacked
and the garden put to bed,
we do nothing

except bear witness
to the spectacle. The sumac
catches fire first, its red igniting
the maple's red and yellow,
the aspen's shaking gold.

On those winter days
when there is nowhere to get,
when the sun's low arc
barely clears the treetops
or the air is busy with snow,
we get nowhere,

content to watch the hemlocks
blur in the noonday dusk,
to wonder how our fire finds
another season's warmth and light
in slabs of beech and oak.

On those endless days
in spring and summer
when twilight lingers like
the final bugle-note of taps,
we keep vigil on a bench
beside the lake.

Our garden is planted,
the supper dishes put away.
There is nothing to do,
nowhere to get,

so we sit perfectly still,
observing how the birches
catch light from the water,
how their leaves become words,
how the words become poems.

About the Author:

Milton J. Bates lives in the Upper Peninsula of Michigan. He has published several nonfiction books, most recently *The Bark River Chronicles: Stories from a Wisconsin Watershed* (2012). A Guggenheim Fellow in 1989, he has also held Fulbright lectureships in China and Spain.

Made in the USA
San Bernardino, CA
17 August 2016